Life of a Poet

Patricia Beaudry

ISBN: 1978423705
ISBN-13: 9781978423701

To my readers:

As I write this book, "Life of a Poet," I am finding a growing number of things I am grateful for through the ups and downs of life. Many of you and many experiences have helped build my character. My life has been touched by those of my past and present, and I am thankful to all. I am thankful to my Lord for sticking by my side in all circumstances and my growing faith as the years flow by. Many thanks to all who have walked with and helped me as I write my first book.

Dear Sue,

It is great to have you as a friend.

Love, Pat

Patricia Beaudry

Contents

Life of a Poet
I was a poet,
but did not know it
until later in life.

In The Beginning

"Why were you named Patricia Dora?" I was born on St. Patrick's Day, in Prosser, Washington. If I had been a boy, I would probably have been named Patrick. Dora was my grandmother's middle name. My dad, also, went by his middle name, but I do not. I had my first home in a two-bedroom house, with my parents, Elmer Chester and Anne Evelyn Stilwell and brother, Wesley (age 5) and sister, Evelyn (age 4). We lived in Grandview where my father worked at Darigold making ice cream and butter. I was told my mother baked layer cakes and sent them to work with my father. He put ice cream between the layers and froze the cake before bringing it home to enjoy. I remember playing a toy xylophone in the closet between the two bedrooms. It was my little hide-away.

Johnny Dowdy was a very good neighborhood friend while I was still living in town. He would come over and we would lie on the parlor floor and look at the encyclopedia or roll a ball back and forth to each other. If we did not catch the ball we would go where it was and roll it back even if it was in another room. In the summer I would go over to his place and we would look at comic books under a weeping willow tree. That was our hide out. He was a year older than I, so he was probably reading by then. His father was my principle and his mother my second grade teacher. I often wonder where Johnny is.

I was terrified in a near car accident when my father hit the shoulder of the road to avoid getting hit by an oncoming car. I was six when it happened on the way to visit my uncle Herm. Our car was left resting above a steep cliff. My father pulled us out the high side, and we crossed the road to wait for help. I was shaking like a leaf and suspect it was the beginning of my stuttering. Special education classes during high school helped me understand the situation and I was told singing would be helpful, because you don't stutter when you sing. I continued to stutter until, in 1971, when I started selling Avon. With the help of a great manager and products to focus on, I was able to say "good bye" to stuttering.

I was amazed to see sweet peas growing along the road on my first trip to western Washington to see Uncle Herm at Lake Crescent. I remember spending a night at a motel and the walls were so thin we could hear people in the next room. I kind of remember there was a small hole in the wall. Here we are standing by the motel.

When we spent the night at Uncle Herm's – where he was caretaker at the Lake Crescent Resort -- my mother, sister and I slept in one full-size bed. I felt like a sardine, because I was in the middle. We had watermelon for breakfast (which was a new time for me). We always ate our watermelon later in the day at home. While there I remember walking past the row of little cabins and having my brother and sister tell me there was a bear hiding in a cabin.

My Chicken House Home

During World War II, my father found a way to move us to the country by building a chicken house as a home (lumber was rationed). We lived there for seven years before our three-bedroom house was built. The chicken house was 24 x 24 feet with a cement floor. We had running cold water and hot water when the wood cook stove was in use. With no drainage, we had to dash the waste water out the back door from a bucket. A shanty behind the garage took care of out toilet needs. At night I used a potty (chamber pot). Saturday night baths were taken in a round galvanized tub by the heating stove behind a clothes rack for privacy. When our grandparents next door got an indoor bathroom, we kids would go over to use their bathtub.

Mother sewed gunny sacks together to divide the sleeping area from the living area. Dressers divided the sleeping areas between my brother and father on one side and my mother and sister in the big bed and I in my six-year crib on the other side. When I outgrew the crib, Mother went to sleep with Dad and I moved in with my sister. I thought we were really up-scale when we had wooden closets built between the two sleeping areas.

A chimney in the middle of the house served two stoves. A cook stove on one side and a heating stove on the other side. I got the job cleaning out the ashes in the stoves after they cooled. I learned to make baking powder biscuits in the cook stove from a Crisco mix recipe from my first cookbook.

Shelves under the chimney held things for the dining table. They became nests when the chickens moved in. Mother made curtains and aprons out of flour sacks. I learned to iron and sew in this home and I remember playing games on the floor. We probably did not have a rug on the floor, because I ordered information about making rugs at a factory from old woolen clothing. I remember playing jacks, Lincoln Logs and Pick up Sticks there.

While still living in the chicken house, my dad built a larger one to raise chickens to produce hatching eggs. We had to carry a stick with us to ward off the roosters when we went out in the barnyard. My dad broke the leg of a rooster when it chased me up onto the haystack. With milk cows, we sold cream to Darigold. Home grown meat and produce kept us well fed. We would butcher and freeze meat for the locker each year.

Mom planted bulbs along the south side of the house and a clothesline hung behind the shanty. With a wringer washer and no dryer, our clothes were often freeze-dried in the winter. A willow tree stood outside the back door and corn was husked there even after we moved into the big house.

After the chickens moved out, Wesley, my brother cleaned it up and made a photography studio. I sewed the backdrop drapes and curtains for the windows. This was where he developed, enlarged, and printed my first wedding pictures he took and put in a lovely photo album as our gift.

Later, the chicken house, with added bathroom, was turned into a hired help residence. The house still stands to this day with an attached carport. That makes four purposes for one building.

Being the adventurous person I was, I slept in the basement in several locations, the upstairs in each room and two places in the living room while the big house was being built. When my brother moved into his completed bedroom, it was no longer fun, so I went back to sleeping with my sister.

It was in the big house I became interested in words. My mother described Mount Adams looking like a "big strawberry ice cream cone" in the rising sunlight. The only other word I remember before then was "baby." I was the youngest of three kids and was referred to as "baby." This had a negative impact on me, as being helpless and dependant.

"What a funny looking Christmas tree." We did not have room for one when we lived in the chicken house, so when we moved into the big house we were happy to have a big window to put the tree in front of. Even though we had no lights to put on it, we went ahead and decorated it with all the ornaments and tinsel to later have our music teacher give us a string of lights. What a mess we made putting the lights on with all the tinsel in the way. Far too much work to take it all off to put the lights on. We learned always to put the lights on first.

Evelyn, my sister, and I had a tradition of waking up Christmas morning and finding a small gift from a friend and taking it back to bed to open. The house was cold for the fire had not been stoked, but the bed was nice and warm. We had to wait for our grandparents to come before we could open the rest of the presents. It was so good to have a big house we could scamper around. I could make a circular path from one room to another. There were a lot of things to be thankful for our first Christmas in our big house. No more trips to grandparents to bathe or outhouse to visit.

Oh the smell of green grass. It was likely before we had a lawn, because I remember lying on a blanket in the pasture by the canal working on a math workbook or relaxing. What a peaceful place with no distractions. After moving to the big house, I had the job of polishing the ornate legs of the dining room tables, because I was small enough to scoot around them.

One day we came home to find a black dog, with brown spots over his eyes, sitting on our back porch. We could not find the owner, so he became our dog. We named him Buster. He was not a very big dog and we were surprised when he brought home a heavy pressure saucepan. It must have had some goodies in it for him to carry it home. We never found where he got the saucepan, so we turned it into a watering bowl, because the weight made it not scoot around. Buster would always be sitting at the back step when we got home from church. He was a very nice farm dog.

Winter was always a fun time when I was growing up. It was the only time I remember my brother, sister and I playing together. We had a sled I loved to play on. We had several hills we would slid down. There was a canal or creek at the bottom of some, so we would flip the sled, so it would not go in. What water that was left in the canal would freeze over in our long cold winters. Wesley would saw a hole in the ice to see if it was thick enough to play on. One day we had a freezing rain on top of several inches of snow. I was able to slide up hill with a running start. I remember coming in and warming up by the stove when my hands got cold, even with gloves.

Faith Journey

My faith journey started out growing up in a Christian home and attending Sunday School sitting around a kidney shaped table listening to Bible stories. Many times the teacher would tell stories with figures stuck to a flannel board. When I got a little older, my restless self got my arm stuck in the rungs of a chair back. With help I was set free. Our family sat in front of my grandparents, in a two-seater pew in the back corner of the church. As I got older, I decided to sit on the other side of the church where I could watch the organist. Then there was Methodist Youth Fellowship (MYF) each Sunday evening and church camp, riding in the back of a truck sitting on our bedroll or luggage. One Sunday, when I was taking communion with the youth, I felt filled with the Holy Spirit.

I attended the Women's Society of Christian Service meetings with my mother when I was young, and was president of the Prosser group when it became United Methodist Women in 1968 when the Methodist Church united with the Evangelical United Brethren Church to become the United Methodist Church. During this time, I spearheaded the formation of Prosser Church Women, a gathering of women from several different local churches. We planned a spring luncheon each year.

My faith continued to grow as I studied at Lutheran Bible Institute and came to love the Word of God. In 2000, as explained in Life Changing Experience, later in the book, I had a big boost to my faith.

Late Teens and On

When I was old enough, I tied, hoed and picked our grapes, picked fruit for my grandfather, babysat for people one third a mile away, and cut asparagus one half mile away. My brother, sister and I rose before sunup to cut asparagus, walk home and take a shower, before catching the school bus. I attended school all 12 years in Grandview. At our class reunion, there were about a dozen of us who had gone all the way through school together.

When I was 20 years old, I had my first of five detached retina. I was standing on a ladder picking cherries, holding onto a limb with one hand and picking with the other. The limb slipped from my hand and almost knocked me off of the ladder. It didn't, but I jerked my head enough to start the detachment. I was seeing spots when I went home for lunch, so my dad took me to the optometrist. After examining my eye, he sent me to see a specialist in Pasco. In two days I was totally blind in that eye before having surgery, and laid on my back for two weeks until it healed. I was not to look down, so I felt the ground with my feet and looked in the distance to get my bearings. When I was allowed to look down, I was told to never do anything that would be a jolt to my head, like riding a horse, diving into water or riding bouncy things. I was very subject to detachment, because I was very near-sighted. This puts a strain on the retina. Thank God for successful eye surgeries.

After graduation from Grandview High, I attended Yakima Valley Junior College for almost two years. My Grandpa Fetterolf died while I was a student. I interrupted my education to help care for my dad, since my mother went to stay with her mother next door. It was too much for my mom to look after both of them.

Husband #1

Who would ever think an old dude ranch would be the place of a budding romance. Labor Day weekend of 1958, I was hiding from my boyfriend, Jack, by the creek at Lazy F Singles Camp, when Lowell Miller came sliding down the bank and introduced himself. That fall he came to work on my mother's washing machine. I sat on the boot box visiting with him. I thought, *Is that him or his father.* I didn't remember him being that bald. When Christmas came there was a beautiful card and hanky in the mail. I sent him a thank you card and later in spring I sent a note to ask if he was going to the Memorial Day singles camp. With an affirmative reply, I asked if Marilyn, a former college roommate, and I could ride with him. I sat in the middle of the front seat with my tin of spice cupcakes. You have heard it said, "The way to a man's heart is through his stomach." It must have worked, because we were soon dating. Our first date was to a car race and the second was to the rodeo.

By the time I married Lowell in 1959, the old church in Grandview (above) I grew up in was replaced with a new one. That was where we got married. My parents opposed me marrying a man 17 years my senior, so we started writing our invitations. When they saw we were determined, they had invitations printed and a wedding cake ordered. I made my lace over satin wedding dress with V-neck and bridal point sleeves with button marching down the back. I transferred my membership to the Prosser Methodist Church where I was very active. We made our first home in a basement apartment in Prosser. Our next home we built between Prosser and Grandview along the highway on land we received as a wedding present from Lowell's parents.

Son, David was born November 1960, the day before Thanksgiving, so Lowell had two dinners: one at the hospital and one at his parents. I was in the hospital for two days before David was born, because labor pains quit and the doctors wanted to watch me more closely, since I had recently had surgery for detached retina. It was sad my father died earlier that year. I think he would have enjoyed having another grandson. On the farm, we had a milk cow, pigs, and chickens. David got a horse after he was old enough to ride. His boyfriends enjoyed coming to the farm to ride his Appaloosa. When David was 11, I started selling Avon products. My sales were good enough to be in the Presidents Club for five years and received many prizes. I, also, sold Fuller Brush and Luzier, a line of cosmetics.

Odd Christmas Tree

On the farm one year, we butchered a cow just before Christmas, so we had all the variety meats. Lowell cut a board the shape of a Christmas tree. I covered it with foil. I cooked the tail, tongue, and heart. I put the tail in the center for the trunk of the tree, sliced the tongue as the ground, sliced heart for the limbs and used mounds of mashed potatoes topped with peach halves as the ornaments on the tree. Unknown to our guests, I had the main meat in the oven. The rest of the food was on the table. When everyone was seated, I passed the tray around, so people could help themselves. What looks I got when they thought that was all they were going to get to eat. After all was served, I brought out the meat from the oven. I don't remember if it was turkey or ham. Since no one ate the tail, I later made Ox Tail Soup, my brother-in-law's favorite. A good time was had by all.

Our Business

Lowell was fired after working for Killingstad Brothers for many years as their appliance repairman. We both sold Fuller Brush while we took a year to build our own business, Miller Repair Service. We constructed our building on our property on Highway 12 between Prosser and Grandview to house our appliance and electronic repairs. Within a short time our business expanded to include a Whirlpool dealership. Lowell built television test equipment and I got the job of testing tubes. I kept the books, ordered parts, did billing, scheduling, firing and hiring. When we moved our business to Prosser to be able to become RCA dealers, I did the displays and advertising. We leased a building in the middle of town, tore down the false ceiling, built scaffolding to paint the high ceiling and built dividers to separate the showroom from the work space. We had one full time employee, part-time delivery and bookkeeper assistant. David worked for us a year between college and the United States Air Force.

College

Thirty years after I dropping out of Yakima Valley Junior College in my sophomore year, I attended Columbia Basin College (CBC). I got a big kick out of the young students coming to me for help in the computer class. They thought I knew everything; I just figured it out. While I was a student there, I went on a Fashion Merchandising Tour to New York City. What a great experience to be able to go into the factories where it is off limits to the public. I bought several yardages of fabric with the hopes of starting a clothing manufacturing business for long-armed women. If men can have sleeve length/collar size, why can't women have bust/arm length measures.

It was during my studies at CBC in Pasco, Washington that I wrote the first poem, "Ode II D Philodendron" in a drawing class. The instructor told us if we did not take the time to do a good job drawing a philodendron in front of a mirror, we were to write a two-page paper telling why. It was before I had one of my many eye surgeries, so I could not tell which was the reflection and which was not. We were to draw the philodendron in color and the reflection in black and white. Following is what I turned in with a title page with a drawing of a philodendron leaf.

Ode II D Philodendron

Oh, Philodendron your vines entwining,
and heart shaped leaves of green and yellow.
To me you hide your magic shapes
all here and there, where do you turn?
Your reflections are they or are they not?
I do not know of which thou art.

My mind confused, my hand frustrated,
my picture becomes a mess of confusion.
My mind wonders to contrived designs.
My hand cannot deceive the beauty God created.
To me your beauty, Oh, Philodendron
to share and care for and not to duplicate.

For some the talent to duplicate,
I admire, but do not share.
I feel the need to create
a design whether practical or not.

Now to my teacher great,
I pray his illness I did not precipitate.
He missed a day, I hope no more,
his guidance is really needed.

Get on we might, my pen and I
distressed to make this two pages long.
My it looks like I should've doubled spaced.
My mind could create much better behind
the steering wheel than at my desk.

Oh, Halloween, your treat to share,
the day of surgery, my vision to repair.
Will be a joy none to compare.
To see again, that gift from God.

The previous poem was written before Lowell passed away
February 15, 1992. Hence the beginning of a flurry of poems. It
was therapeutic.

Spring 1992

I set me down, with pen in hand
        to share with you my thoughts.
This Easter day shines forth with hope
        for those been touched by Christ.

The sun shines warm, the dogwood blooms,
        God's message to us all,
that life with him has new beginnings,
        for all who believe in Him.

Now for me, my home may change
        before the summer has past.
In hand I have an earnest for
        to others my home may have.

Then where to me my hat to hang,
        be it to rent or to buy.
A new home I will make,
        with you I hope to share

What job I find I know not where,
        before my roots go deep.
I know dear God my side you'll be
        where ever I must go.

And now I ask you show to me
    the path I must trod.
My restless heart yearns this day
    for a new life to have with Thee.

For a New Life to Have with Thee

Now I sit amongst these boxes,
    wondering what to toss or save.
Thirty-two years, three bedrooms full,
    some forgot, much long since used.

Now this yard sale up to come,
    easier I hope the weight to bear.
Hard to let the past to go,
    so soon the grief of loved one past.

Soon the job I'm hoping for,
    their choice of me I know not yet.
A stepping stone I wish it is,
    of more my needs to fulfill.

Lord, guide me in my thoughts and deeds,
    these days ahead my life you lead.
I ask for strength this day and on
    to a fuller life with Thee begin.   *Summer 92*

This was a time in my life when I had much to think about. I need to discover what my new self would be. Many decisions about how to dispose of equipment and supplies from our business. Some test equipment went to a trade school. How I was going to support myself, where to live and what I was to do with the farm. I eventually sold the farm after moving to town and going back to college a third time. Oh, so many changes. I never would have believed how everything has turned so amazing.

The next two poems were written after I moved from my three-bedroom country home to a one-bedroom apartment in Prosser. Space was tight but did suffice. I lived down the street from my sister-in-law and enjoyed walking the neighborhood.

Changes

Another year will soon be past,
    many changes since last we met.
Now to tell you what they were,
    of many more to unfold.

As my husband slowly wasted away,
    many birds my hands created.
By his side I quietly waited,
    as our Lord to him did call.

Lonely hours and much to ponder –
    I tried my best to sort the past.
Soon I thought my place was sold,
    but snatched it back to rent instead.

Then to town indeed I moved,
    in a one bedroom pad I squeezed.
Still the boxes set for sorting
    of which to keep or part I wondered.

Two yard sales I parted much,
    of 32 years we did collect.
Much more to part before I sell
    to others my home posses.

New work found to replace loves income –
    the care of elders I give to some.
Their lonely hours I do share
    and meals I joyfully prepare.

Oh! I most forgot, my wheels I changed,
 for now I drove a red Isuzu.
The mileage better I do obtain,
 do hope to save for new horizons.

Now to this poem I hope it to be
 part of a book of poems by me.
These many months of solitude brings
 new beginnings of which we see.

Now my address you see has changed,
 I hope you will use it to bring me joy.
With this I wish you a merry Christmas.
 May God bless you with much joy.

???

Questions, questions, and more questions.
 Where do they all come from?
Always questions to answer.
 Always answers to find.

What is it where is it, when will it come?
 What do I look for first
a job, a house or some kind of wheels?
 Always wondering what comes first.

Where will a job for me be?
 Will it be near or be it far?
This I must find before a home I make.
 For that I would not uproot again.

What will I be when I grow up?
 Will I work for thee or me?
Your benefits I would like,
 Your corset I would not.

Where oh where will I find myself?
 When oh when will it be?
Always wondering who I am,
 And where my path will go?

School-- will it be the door to my future?
What shall I learn, what shall I do?
Always listening, always looking,
for that clue to guide me on.

Now for this mess, I must confess,
some day to combat before I part.
What do I keep, what do I throw?
Of which to part with I do not know.

Now who wants this and who wants that?
Wait too long or it be gone.
You must decide, so I can proceed.
This mess I must dismantle.

The day I do look forward to,
a new horizon on which to bloom.
The grief of past behind,
the new tomorrows beckoning.

Dear Lord, these very steps I take,
your help I greatly need.
Your guidance I ask, your way to show,
my path to me this day.

The time does fly, where does it go?
too often lost in a daze.
My purpose be, I hope to see,
before my days are past.

Now guide me, Lord, this day is over,
To rest with you in slumber blest.
My dreams be sweet, remember next
on that which you provide.

This poem was written in thanks for the many gifts I received my first Christmas as a widow.

Many Thanks

Many thanks to all I give
  for gifts galore with me you shared.
For food, things of beauty or to read
   and pictures of my recent Virginia trip.

Now the turkey its bones appearing --
  many dishes I hope to prepare
with morsels of meat still remaining,
  with others I hope to share.

Then back to work I go, at church and home
  and with others my care I share.
My thoughts are full of love you gave to me.
  My thanks to you this day with love.

The next poem was written to honor and thank the workers who kept the streets free of snow. It was published in the Prosser Herald.

Dappled Snow

Dappled with snow the hills proudly stand,
    waiting for spring to burst forth with green.
Long lay the winter, cold upon the earth,
    blanketing green shoots soon forth to rebirth.

Slowly now the snow does melt,
    long it lay upon the ground.
Lost the joy in children's eyes
    when first the snow was new.

Many the times the blade did pass,
    to open our way to work and school.
Gravel then lay where last was snow,
    the white mountains did grow and grow.

Sweepers now the blades replaced,
    prepared for spring and cleaner streets.
Many the hours the workers shoved and scooped
    the beautiful blanket that once was there.

Now may our hearts within us rest
    and think of how we've been so blest.
We only know that time will tell
    how God again will bring spring back.

The following poem was written after a balloon came loose from the string on the way to the Prosser cemetery to place it on my husband's grave.

Straightway

Straightway to heaven the balloon did float,
    the one I bought for my husband dear.
The grave bypassed, the walk cut short,
    to watch the balloon so swiftly rise.

Quickly my neighbor did turn to catch
    the sky-bound balloon its mission to do.
Quietly we watched as heaven bound it went
    to the one I miss since one year he passed.

This poem was sent to my brother and sister to honor our mother who had passed away January 1983.

To My Mother's Children

On this special day, let us remember Mother dear,
    of all the love and caring she humbly gave.
As she shared her love of our Lord Jesus,
    a wondrous example for all to follow.

The gentle touch and guidance she gave
    to her children and to any in need.
Warm and happy was the home we shared
    which she and Daddy made for us.

Now let our hearts to them give thanks
    for all the many fond memories.
Have many more "Happy Mother's Days"
    'till above we all shall meet.

    With love from little sister,
      Pat Miller, 5/93

The following poem was written in response to an artistic drawing of a cross I found in the pew as I did one of my Monday morning duties as secretary.

Crossroads

Here is the cross, the cross you left for me,
    the cross that makes the difference
        between life and the world of cares.

Now I gladly share this cross, it's burden gladly bear.
    In the crossroads now I stand,
        ready my life I turn to thee.

Where the road leads I know not where.
    I trust dear Lord your guidance give
        the direction you have for me.

Now to my friends I soon will leave.
    I give God's blessing for your safety.
        I am so glad we shared God's crossroads.

Moving On

I was on the communication committee of the Prosser church when they were looking for a secretary. I said, "I will do the communication project, if you give me the job of church secretary." I got the job and worked under two pastors. As I sorted the mail one day, I saw that the Sunnyside United Methodist Church was looking for a secretary. I applied and interviewed with high quality newsletter in hand, and got the job. While working there, I read about a Prayer and Healing Conference in Issaquah at Lutheran Bible Institute. I asked the pastor for an extra day off, so I could attend. During breaks, as I walked the halls, I read posters and brochures. I thought, *Is this where God wants me to be?* I called to inquire when I got home and soon had my application in the mail. I was accepted one week before classes, so I hurriedly sold, gave away or put into storage the rest I did not want to take with me. David and I loaded both of our cars and headed off to college. I soon found my room in student housing was too cramped and noisy with all the young students. So I paid extra for a room in the married student wing. I had a large room with full bath and large closet. Thanks for the peace and quiet.

Biblical Overture

Here I am at LBIS, walking with my friends
through "the garden" in all its glorious splendor.
I walk with others through Pentateuch and Luke/Acts,
the stories telling the message so glorious.

Moses did write these first five books, Pentateuch it is.
In Genesis, Exodus, Leviticus, Numbers and Deuteronomy
he tells the stories of our ancestors.
This Biblical Overture to be heard for eternity.

"In the beginning God created" and there we had our start.
For many descendants God did bless them.
Through grumbling and groaning God stood by their side.
His grace freely given, though often not accepted.

Now God did guide them, by Moses command,
the people of Israel fled their bondage in Egypt.
With ten plagues God convinced Pharaoh to
"let my people go" to a "land of milk and honey."

In the wilderness the redeemed people wandered,
being tested as oft we are in our own lives.
Though grumble they did, God never failed them.
For God's promise is "I will be with you."

In the ten commandments God gave to Moses
we find our guide for daily life,
that we may not wander beyond His protective arms,
a shield to always protect us from harm.

We worship you now, O Lord, as you see fit.
As you came to us in dedication, service and fellowship,
we now come to you in repentance asking for forgiveness,
that we may feast in fellowship and come to thee in service.

As we see the "foreshadow of Christ" in the Old Testament,
through study may we come to know the Bible more clearly.
May we come to thee, O Lord, thankful and with dedication,
and through our witness of Christ be of service to Thee.

*Comments from my LBI teacher: "Thanks Pat" You have
remembered a lot of good tidbits from our study. Keep it up.
Indicated as a poem for XC.*

The following poem came to me during the night after a troubling
experience. It is David's favorite poem of mine.

Lead Me

Oh Lord, you lead me all the days of my life.
Though I may stumble, you pick me back up.
Many the trials you put me through.
Many the insights they bring forth to me.

Many the words to my mind you impart,
during the night when the window you open.
Down on paper the words must go,
for where pen and paper meet, the psalm has its start.

The spring of 1994, while attending college, found me reeling from
all the losses over the last couple of years: no longer a wife with
the death of my husband, no longer a home or business owner, no
longer a Prosserite, and no longer part of the church family of
which I was a member for 32 years. To top it off, a councilor
recommended I break off a dear friendship. As a result of these
losses, I ended up in the psych ward at Overlake Hospital. I don't
know what I'd have done without my Christian faith to back me up
at that time.

Since I was unable to get the classes I wanted at Bellevue
Community College and find suitable housing, my son invited me
to come live with him in Lynnwood, Washington. When I first
moved in, I slept on the floor until he could get a two-bedroom

apartment. Having always having dinner prepared when he came home from work, I enjoyed sharing time and space with him.

This next poem was written and sent to friends and relatives, telling of my new address and changes made.

Home Again

My home again, now I have changed,
    different town, different setting.
Now to share David's apartment
    while I get myself back together.

Spent some time in the hospital
    to get some help to lift my spirits.
Better now with medication,
    looking forward to a new lease on life.

Different schooling I am trying,
    computer classes and empowerment strategies.
Edmonds College in Lynnwood is where it is,
    just down the street by bus or car.

Got some leads to possible jobs,
    not real anxious, but know I must.
Work will get me out and purpose to be
    a worker in God's world to fit His will.

Many the times your name brings to me
    memories of times together we've been.
Let not the miles and circumstances us part,
    but keep in touch by mail or phone.

Now my address you can see
    has changed to Lynnwood, Washington.
Check the return upon the envelope.
    Hope to hear from you real soon.

The Rhythm of Life

"Hello world." I am here to learn
    the meaning of life – just why I am here.
To Mother's womb, I said, "Good bye."
    This world is now my home.

Hello family, I am growing tall,
    my babyhood I leave behind.
We share and love each other here,
    at home in our greenhouse of life.

Now as I grow, my interests broaden.
    Good bye to home and family dear.
Hello world and institutions of learning.
    I am here to learn God's plan for my life.

Years pass me by and loved ones too
    from this life into the next.
I trust dear Lord you will lead me next
    to other "Hello"s and doors of life.

The rhythm of life – "Hello"s and "Good byes"
    there's many we have in our travel through life.
When our time has come for our last "Good bye"
    we can be assured God has the last "Hello."

The next several poems were written while attending a poetry class at the University of Washington, July and August of 1994. I really enjoyed being encouraged to expand my style of writing.

Time

Time is the space between two points,
Equally given and equally received.
How you use it is up to you--
squandered away or honorably filled.

T is for times I spent with you.
I is for "I long to be with you again."
M is for mothers we all received.
E is for "Every day is a new beginning."

Now how is the time you have spent?
Does it make you smile or make you cry?
Is it not great we have another chance?
For today is the day you can have a new start.

Instructor's comments: Good, I like positive poem with lots of hope *in them. MH*

For the next poem we were to pick five words we liked the sound of and write a poem around it. I chose horizontally, vertically, merrily, fledgling and guarantee.

In Flight

Merrily the fledgling soared above the nest,
in graceful lines above the horizon.
Horizontally it glided from tree top to tree top.
With much practice success is guaranteed.

With much practice the fledgling became most skilled.
For now it can dive vertically to catch its food.
Oh, the joy to fly where one wishes,
to merrily view the horizon and dream of a new day.

Barbell Bummer

Bulgingly the biceps slowly rose
at a greater height than times before.
Sweat dripping down and face in a grimace
barbell bummer gave it all he had.

A stevedore by trade he was
'til drugs he used and then got fired.
Now weight lifting competition was his bag
in hopes of winning the mounting stakes.

He had no family, friend or foe,
only the bottle and a spot under the bridge.
Wishing to win so a room he could get,
and leave the bottle behind and win back a heart.

This poem was written as a special assignment in the poetry class.

The Rocky Rain

The rocky rain came spattering down,
upon the muddy meadow.
The pebbles hit hard upon the pond
'till all was left, a heap of rocks.

Now where did the water go?
Up to the sky on light blue wings.
Down in a crystal state this time,
White upon white 'til all came to a halt.

Now where did the snow a fleeting go,
when sunshine sang it far away.
Gone to earth to feed the flowers,
for another season of beauty and glory.

A Pin and a Song

A pin and a song brought tears to my eyes.
A pin and a song brought back memories
of a friend and a conversation with him
when my spirits were low and I asked for the end.

The pin I wore said, "I am loved."
The song I sang said, "Jesus loves me.
this I know, for the Bible tells me so."
as in my youth the song I did learn.

"Little ones to him belong"
and you and I if we believe,
that God to earth did send his Son
to make our sins as white as snow.

"I am weak, hut He is strong,"
so the song does tell us so.
"Little ones to Him belong,"
and you and I, if we just ask.

Much of my writing took place at night when inspiration would grab me out of sleep.

Sleepless in Bed

Restless legs,
   mind's no better,
      just can't sleep.
         What's the matter?
Diet Pepsi,
   too much food,
      mind excited,
         so much happening.
Job a looking,
   Bible studying
      new friends making,
         What's coming next?
New home maybe,
   if job gotten,
      far from here
         if God willing.
So now written
   this new morning,
      let mind rest
         'til sun comes shining.
Good night morning,
   beddy bye computer,
      save some lines,
         for another day.

Silent Dreams

Silently stealing across my mind,
pictures of grandeur and pain gone by.
Hide from my mind the pain of the past
and give me new hope of a grander day.

Oh dreams of darkness, give light and guidance.
Let the good overshadow the not so good.
How real you can be, like the dream I dreamt,
I woke with a start to catch my tripping step.

Dreamt in my youth on my pillow did crawl
a spider much bigger each time I swiped it away.
Finally I woke madly swiping away
at the spider so big you ever did see.

Another childhood dream – the reappearing red bull
would chase me into the canal without its watery grave.
Much like the rooster who chased me upon the haystack
while my stick kept getting shorter as I swatted away.

Much grander were the dreams when
I could fly or walk upon pillows of air.
Oh such fun to soar over all or walk
with dancing steps on pillows of air.

Now dreams of the past and dreams of the future,
hang onto the good and throw away the rest.
May the longings of the heart bring hope for the future
and dreams that will bring a smile to my face.

Love

Oh heart so gently warmed and calm,
      my breath so long and steady.
The love I feel, O God, to share
      with one for whom I dearly care.

Lord lead me in thy path today,
      my life to you I give.
You know my heart and soul within.
      your love to those I wish to share.

Instructor's comments: I like the optimism and sense of hope here. MH

Love Everlasting

Love is the intangible thing from God,
unmeasured and temperature unrecorded.
Its warmth felt and is all encompassing,
to all given and meant to be shared.

When is it shared, but with a smile,
a kind word, and a need fulfilled.
God gave to all, but not for to keep.
Only when shared are we fully blessed.

The love God showed when his Son he gave,
to cleanse us from sin, if only we believe.
Now to share the love with those around,
and know that God's love has no end.

A Token

I needled and hooked away today
at this token of love I made for you.
You shared of your home and of your heart
to one as lost as the wide open sea.

My days made better with your smiles of care.
My hope restored for God came to us in love.
May we never forget there are others out there
who need the same love you showed to me.
Now Christmas does come but once a year,
but memories of you come back time and again.
May joy and peace fill your heart all year long
'till we meet again at God's own choosing.

Christmas '94

Christmas is near and many cards to go
to friends and family the miles do us part.
Wishes of peace, of happiness and health
do come your way on this gray rainy day.

Hope comes from light, the light from God's love,
in His son Jesus who came to us on Christmas day.
May the joy of the babe's birth in the manger
bring peace to your heart both now and for years to come.

May the peace I have found in studying the Word
show forth in my life and bring others that hope.
For in Christ there's love to share with those around us,
not just at Christmas, but all the year long.

Heart to Heart

Valentine's Day comes once a year,
    but love is ours from day to day.
God sent his Son so all may receive
    his love to us, a most precious gift.

The love received is meant to be shared.
    For only then do we get the full reward.
May the love that Christ brings to us,
    Bring peace and happiness to your life.

Though the miles may be many that do us part,
    the thoughts of you bring warm memories.
My best wishes to you I send this day
    with God's love from me to you.

Happy Valentine's Day

The next poem was written about my Disciple I class of friends lead by Ginny Scribner. I still meet with several of the women in various bible studies.

Circle of Friendship

The circle of friendship grows and grows.
Its knitting grows tighter and arms reach farther.
The weeks and months we studied together
brings new understanding of God's message.

Disciple class, most ably led by Ginny,
was the place we prayed and studied together.
We shared concerns and insights, too,
in our walk with our Lord, 'tis Jesus Christ.

Our classmates remembered with rings and cards,
when traveling Jan to Jamaica did cruise.
Many the times our prayers and call did lift
Connie and others whose faith was well tested.

Now as the class comes to a close,
we turn our eyes outward to look for God's will.
Our lives and our faith we must share with others,
for it is then we are the hands of Christ.

Once Again

Once again my address changed.
A yearly trek I seem to take.
Now a home I gladly share
with Marguerite, that is her name.

David has parted to other places.
Left me there to pack again
all the stuff I still possess,
from years gone by and still a stackin'.

Now the path that brought me here
is at times a bit confusing.
Six jobs later, I hope the last
the place God wants for me.

From sales, to research and condo setting, too,
the best thus far was the elder care I gave.
But then the door opened to a church down south,
that was looking for a secretary at Ronald UMC.

Just when I get happy with my stage in life,
my Lord seems to call at another door.
For if you knew my past, you would surely know,
nothing stays the same but change itself.

The Bible I pursue from time to time.
Daily readings I try to do.
From college classes to Disciple, too,
I'm really hooked on the Holy Word.

Now where my life goes from here on out,
Only God knows his blessings to bestow.
Working, reading, writing, and sharing a life,
what more could I ask, God thank you for all.

To all with whom my paths have crossed,
a blessing to me your life did impart.
Again I hope another chance
To share God's love with all so dear.

This next poem was included in a Senior Singles secret gift at a Christmas gift exchange. My pen name was used to cover my identity. At the time I was selling Avon, so the gift was hand cream.

Hand it to You

My gift to you I hand to you
to soften and to dry.
The hands you have, God gave to you
to serve in all you do.

Now I do care, most deeply care
your Christmas filled with joy.
The love God gave for all to share
on the first Christmas long ago.

We share some time together here
each month one Sunday the first to come.
Now other times we are apart,
but in our hearts we are together.

Padora Stiller

A Song

Dear God, you told me to write
    the messages you give to me.
I wait until the time is right,
    but swift you kick
when on my duff I sit.

Stubbornly I wait for that bit of inspiration,
    my mind so full—no room to listen.
You speak to me when least I expect it,
    when pain and grief does prick my heart.

The song recalls a friend I have.
    In Jesus I can always trust.
When once was sung at my love's farewell
    This precious song of a friend forever be.

The tears it brought of memories past.
    My long lost love you do replace.
Your comfort and friendship will always be,
    If only I come to thee in prayer.

The following poem was printed on fancy paper, laminated and given to an older couple and to my granddaughter for her August 2017 wedding.

Two Become One

Two shoe strings become a bow.
Two socks become a pair.
Two feet in one direction go.
Two legs a burden equally share.
Two eyes see one image.
Two ears hear one message.
Two knees on which one prays,
thank God for all these twos.

Two hands become a hand shake.
Two for tea, just wait and see.
Meeting eyes, an open window,
speaks to the depth of the heart.

Two arms become an embrace.
Two lips become a kiss.
Two ears hear one message,
God's love and that of a lover.

Man and woman with wedding vows
become "one" for their life to come.
God bless you both with joy and peace.
The one you chose—a gift from God.

First Cruise

It was in the late 1990's, when I went on my first cruise with my friend, Elaine Stewart (now deceased). She is on the right in this picture.

NORWEGIAN **M/S DREAMWARD**

This was a writers cruise to the Eastern Caribbean. When we were at sea, we were in classes. And when in port, we went ashore. I was much younger then and was able to get around to take many pictures of the sights we saw. A favorite thing about the cruise was the Afterglow gatherings in the evening, when we shared our favorite books, movies, authors, etc.

It was interesting to talk with other writers and keep in touch for some time afterwards. From our dinner table we overlooked the pool and it was fun to see the water splashing around when the seas were a little rough. And the food was really great. Our itinerary was switched from the Western Caribbean because of storms. We were given sea-sick pills when we boarded, but I did not take them after the first day, because they put me out. I rather have had a good excuse to walk like a drunken sailor.

Before flying home, we visited a wildlife park in the Everglades and rode an airboat to see the alligators. I was the first person to spot one. All in all it was a very fun trip. It was fun to meet other writers and get to know them. I kept in touch with our dinner partners for some time.

Life Changing Experience

July 2000 I traveled as a homeless person for a month through parts of Washington and Oregon. I chose to become homeless because my rent went up $75.00 and it was taking too much of my income. I felt God's call to become closer to Him and to gain a better understanding of what homeless people experience. During my travels I lived on a budget of $30.00 a day for food, transportation and lodging.

My faith was tested the first day when I locked my keys and cell phone in the car. I thought, I will go ahead and take a walk. Maybe I will meet someone who has a cell phone I can use. As I calmly proceeded with my planned walk, my prayers were answered with the appearance of a couple from Bellevue on their bicycles. They let me use their phone to contact my insurance company for assistance. Since I was told it would take 1 ½ hours before help would arrive, I finished my walk. In returning to my car I waited the last half hour sitting on a nearby rock. When help didn't come, I flagged down a woman driving a power-company pickup to see if she had a phone I could use. I shared with her the purpose of my journey while being put on hold several times. I met many people to get a better understanding of services available. Within a half hour help arrived to unlock my car. I continued my trip to my brother's home north of Grandview where we grew up. Thanks to the long summer day and helpful people, it was still daylight when I arrived at 8:00 p.m.

I started out in late June at my brother's guest house helping with yard and house work. It helped me keep within my budget by helping others when staying in their home. While there I helped at the Prosser Thrift Store. My timing was well appreciated, because a smiling clerk said "It was one of our busiest Saturdays we have had in some time." My job was to pull and bag clothing that was on the shelves too long. These items were shipped to an agency that sends clothes overseas.

This journey as a homeless gave me an opportunity to visit and help relatives and friends. On the way to Oregon I stopped at my niece, Sharron's home in Vancouver, Washington. It made me feel needed to comfort her daughter during her brief, nasty sick spell.

While spending a couple of days in their home, I went to Portland to visit *Sisters of the Road Café.* This café is run for and by the homeless and low income people. For $1.50 a person can get a hearty nutritious meal. If they don't have money they can work 15 minutes for their meal. Other services for the homeless were job search, help with housing, etc.

After leaving my niece, a visit to an ex-neighbor from Prosser gave her joy as it was her first out of town visitor in 6 ½ years. Then I headed for Corvallis where I spent time with Mae Graham and helped out at the Westminster House Soup Kitchen. I was able to visit with a young homeless man as we shared a meal and he took me on a tour of the college campus across the street. He and some others I met prefer to be homeless.

When I left Mae I headed for Eugene and had my first experience staying at a hostel. It is low cost dormitory style housing with a shared kitchen. Eating picnic lunches out of my ice-chest helped me keep expenses down.

The next two nights in motels stretched my housing budget because I wanted to see Crater Lake. I was delighted to see many more of God's creation: the second highest water falls in Oregon, the brilliant blue of Crater Lake and the delightful Natural Bridge of the Rogue River. After a picnic in a Medford park, I shared my journey experience with two Latter Day Saints missionaries who happened to come by. They were really interested in the Disciple magazine I showed them.

Leaving Medford I returned to Eugene to visit cousin, Arthur. I was thrilled with the music as he played the pipe organ he built. After visiting in their lovely home and eating a delicious dinner prepared by his wife, Carol, I returned to spend two more nights at the Hummingbird Hostel in Eugene. Between the two nights I attended the First United Methodist Church in Eugene and rested and walked in a park. I also checked my email at the library, as I frequently did in other libraries along the way. I often saw homeless people doing the same.

The next day I headed for the coast with a stop at the Oregon Coast Aquarium and visited my cousin, Charlie, who has conquered cancer with medication and a change of diet. After two more nights in cheap motels, I was glad to spend two nights at the Seaside Hostel. I was glad I could leave my bed made up since my planned visit to Pioneer House in Astoria was a side trip. Had I known I was going to be offered a bed at Pioneer House I could have stayed there. While there I did my laundry, had lunch with some homeless ladies and left with a bag of groceries from the director feeling much was being done for the homeless.

I found on my journey there were many reasons for homelessness, some by choice and some not. I found there were many services available. My first line of contact was through various churches and the use of the Internet before I left my friend, Peggy's home.

I met some interesting people at the hostels. There was a mixture of homeless and economy travelers. One I met in Eugene was a "traveling preacher." He knew the Bible and would preach about the end time to all who would listen. One of the usual questions to ask other hostellers was, "where are you going next?' His answer was, "Wherever God leads me." He was still there when I returned after my three-day absence. Wonder if he is still there? God bless him. One never knows how God will use you.

After leaving Seaside I headed back to Portland and spent the night at another hostel. There was an 86 year old woman and a man whom I met at Seaside. He paid me $10.00 to mow the lawn with a push lawn mower. He was doing yard work to help pay his expenses at the hostel.

When I worshipped at the Rockford United Methodist Church the next morning, there was a couple there celebrating their 75th wedding anniversary. It was amazing to see three members of the church holding boards stretching across the sanctuary with 25 candles each. A lovely reception followed.

Back into Washington I visited and helped my sister-in-law in Shelton. Then I spent a night at the Vashon Island Hostel where I met an international traveler who was attending a conference in Seattle.

I finished my journey by spending a night with my college roommate, Marilyn Rice, in Dupont, Washington, before spending a month with Edie Tye taking care of her dog while she worked and preparing meals for us.

What have I learned from this experience? I know you can keep within a budget, if you try. Most of all I know prayer works. I felt the comfort and protection of the prayers of friends and family. I was able to keep calm in two close calls with cars that crowded me off the road. I felt God's protective hand over me. I never felt threatened by all the strangers with whom I talked. I found it is hard work to live and travel as a homeless person. I dropped into different beds exhausted each night. I slept well and God provided for my needs as long as I was willing to do my part. This whole experience made big changes in my life. I wouldn't change it for anything. I went with the "they" and "me" mentality and came back with the notion of "us." People said I was a different person after this journey. With morning and evening devotions and prayer my faith in God was greatly increased.

Alone Again

The most traumatic events in my life occurred when beloved family members passed away. My Grandpa Fetterolf died when I was a student at Yakima Valley Junior College in Yakima, Washington. I interrupted my education to help care for my dad, since my mother had gone to stay with her mother. I did a mix of full-time and part-time studies until my husband's health made it necessary to cut back on my studies.

At my mother's sudden death, I soon realized she had been my connection to the rest of the family and relatives. Her death was doubly hard, realizing at my age of 45 years old, I was now part of the eldest generation of both my family and my husband's family. What a shock to add to the grief!

When my first husband died at age 71, I was left alone to manage the five-acre family farm with no close relatives to help. David lived and worked 30 miles away, so I rented my house and moved from a three-bedroom house to a one-bedroom apartment. What a squeeze!

At the time I worked as secretary for our church. The following spring, I became the secretary of a larger church. While working there, I became aware of a Prayer and Healing Conference at Lutheran Bible Institute in Issaquah. Upon reading posters and brochures during breaks, I felt God wanted me to be there as a student.

After attending college full-time for six months, I moved in with my son in Lynnwood, Washington, via the psych ward to deal with the effects of the many changes in my life. In two years, I had lost my spouse, home, business and life style and community where I'd spent most of my life. I had lost all my identity in continual adjustment.

Through all these experiences, I have found relationships are more important than material goods. With each loss, I was able to gain new skills of filling my needs and asking for help when needed. I praise God for sticking by my side through my life journey.

Home for Christmas

"I'll be home for Christmas, if only in my dreams."
But, as the tears start to form, I say, "Where is home?"
Is it where I was born, where I grew up, where my son grew up?

Or is it one of the many homes since then I have had?

For now my home is where I hang my hat
– a place where I can be me,
A place I can meet with my Lord
and remember the family that makes it home.

My church family has become my home,
a home full of friends too many to count.
So, now when I hear, "I'll be home for Christmas,"
I can think of my church family, who will always be there for me.

So, may we come to our Lord's house,
and say "I am home for Christmas."
Today and all year through,
may the joy of Christmas be with you all.

Husband # 2

I quit counting addresses when I got to #13 on the west side of the Cascade Mountains. Some were apartments, some were home shares, one condo and the home I shared with Richard, my fun-loving husband. I do miss him. One address was a rented office, before I got settled in a home with a disabled lady. I enjoyed living with her, but my room was too small. Then I moved to the bottom floor of a condo I shared with another lovely lady. I had a lot of room there and created a make-do kitchen and washed my dishes in the bathroom sink. I cooked and shared some meals with Katherine upstairs. She was a great candy maker and loved to play games with me.

The long gap in poetry writing was in part due to the gift of a computer from my son (thanks David) and access to the internet. I began to search the internet for Mr. Right. It turned out to be Richard (Dick) Beaudry. Our first meeting in person was Thursday, October 4, 2003 at a potluck at my church. I overslept that morning to wake at 11:40 AM. I hurriedly brushed my teeth, dressed and picked up ice cream on the way, because I figured they would be ready for dessert by the time I got there. Later, Norma told me he asked her, "Where is Pat?" "Pat who?" He answered, "I don't know her last name." After the potluck, we took a tour of the church and exchanged email addresses. He accepted my invitation to Senior Singles luncheon the following Sunday. I told him it would likely be all women, but he came anyway. After lunch, I followed him to his place and had a tour of his two-story home with chair-lift. I thought, *Is this going to be my home?*

I told myself I would never marry him, because he was Catholic. We soon found I was wrong. We were married the following January 17. We had one good year together, then his health started to fail. He died 19 months and two days after we got married. We went to both churches each weekend, and both benefited sharing each other's religions. In fact, he said, "If I was looking for another church, this would be it." He loved Pastor Dave's sermons. Dick brought home the tapes of the worship service each week to copy. We listened to them and a Tennessee Ernie Ford tape when we made a trip to the Midwest.

It was a short, sweet marriage. We were a good match, and he was so much fun. Great times were had in the hot tub and our few trips together. I miss him very much and thank God for the joy he brought into my life. I lived in his house in Mountlake Terrace for another year and a half before buying a condo in north Lynnwood. It was lovely inside, but nothing to do outside the door, so after five years I sold the condo at a loss and moved to Ballinger Court Apartments in Edmonds. I was so appreciative for the many activities. While living there, I wrote the following poem.

No Body is Some Body

You say, "No body is here," but I beg to disagree.
So there must be someone here or I would not tell you so.
There is you and there is me, so that makes at least two.
So don't say, "There is no one here," when you and I are here.
There is always someone here when the question can be asked.
'Cause the asker is someone and so am I.

How Dry I Am

Now look at me, my tail showing,
    My head in this cave I found.
The salt so tasty, 'til I swelled so tight
    My reverse worked no more.

That little light teased me forward,
    'til I was stuck oh so tight.
Now I find myself stuck forevermore,
    Dry as dry as all get out.

This is a dry mouse stuck in the bottom of a salt shaker.

Leaves of Life

Green and gold, you show your faces,
many all gathered together:
one more gold than others,
some blemished, some perfect,
some hiding, some standing out.
Some in pairs march along,
and others in triplets round about.

Now where is the music in my head?
I can not hear it, where did it go?
Who holds you together, but Jesus Christ,
the one who brings unity to the world?

Now every face I see is different,
some more golden than others --
not more brilliant, but more light giving.
Where do you learn, but life itself?
Years pass me by as wisdom grows.

I smell no fragrance in your leaves, but beauty you have.
Some even blush as they peak from behind.
How sturdy you are in diversity – you stand alone,
but in togetherness.
Do your colors change as older you get?
I know not why since we just met.

Preceding was written at a church retreat at Rainbow Lodge

Second Cruise

On Saturday, July 19, 2014 John and Jan Pruatt took Peggy Cousins and me to meet the Holland America Westerdam.

I asked for a wheelchair and had someone push me all the way to our room. Peggy pushed my walker with our carry-on luggage. Our checked luggage was there when we arrived at our room. We missed the Welcome program because I was too tired after attending the emergency drill. Because of a late sign-up, our dinner was at 7:45 p.m.. Neither of us slept well the first night, but did after that except the one night I got seasick.

Sunday we were at sea and enjoyed morning worship with Dr. Charles Stanley and a concert with Babby Mason in the afternoon. I didn't care for her first concert, but the later one I did. Dr. Stanley spoke again after her concert. Then we were treated with a performance by David Pendleton, ventriloquist.

David Pendleton and I

After our late dinner we had the Gospel Music Concert. What a glorious sound unto our Lord. It made for a restful night.

Monday we heard from Andy Stanley, Charles' son. It was interesting to hear how they came to their ministry differently. We arrived in Juneau in the afternoon, but I did not go ashore. Had I asked some questions earlier in the week about accessibility, I might have done so. As was the case most days, we had another great gospel concert after our late dinner. It made for a late night, but we were always greeted with a folded towel creature, chocolates and a saying in another language on our return to our room. Many of the stewards were from the Philippines and other countries. Here is a picture of our last creature. Wish I had taken more pictures of them. They were on our bed each evening when we got back to our room.

Tuesday we visited Glacier Bay. We spent a good hour watching the best calving (when big sheets of ice fall into the water) of the season. It was a beautiful sunny day. Our gospel concert was in the afternoon that day, so we were able to get to bed earlier. We did our personal devotions in the morning and at bedtime.

Wednesday we anchored off of Sitka. Those who went ashore took a tender (a small boat boarded at water level). Instead we attended Geology & Genesis presented by Billy Caldwell followed by another session with Charles Stanley. We skipped the comedy by Dennis Swanberg, because we had seen it the night before on the closed circuit TV.

The only rain we had was early Thursday morning before we went ashore at Kechikan. It was dry before we left the ship. I had help going down the ramp, so I would not go too fast. We went up one side of one block and back the other side of the street, stopping at several shops. I only bought socks, popcorn and something to drink. I sat and rested while Peggy visited the visitors center.

Statue in front of the visitor center.

That afternoon we were presented the gospel music "Christmas Jubilee. It was not all Christmas music, but their props for "Let it Snow" was hilarious. For snow, they blew several rolls of toilet paper over the bass singer. We were sitting down front and I got to be in a snowball fight with them. Oh such fun. After dinner we got to hear from Andy.

Friday we were at sea most of the day and docked at Victoria, BC at 5:30 p.m.. We had a good view from the ship and saw a helicopter land on the heliport. The bookstore was open every day so we could buy CDs, DVDs and books written by the presenters. I would have liked to get all their CDs, but it would have cost too much.

Saturday morning, we arrived to sunny Seattle and left our dream cruise for a waiting taxi. I was welcomed home by my blooming cactus in my hot apartment, and even had enough energy to enjoy a game of bingo with my Ballinger friends.

Music

Music is a big part of my life. I grew up hearing my dad play 'Star of the East' on the piano at bedtime. He could not read music, so played by ear. I had a toy xylophone when I was a little girl and the neighbor had a big one. We used to go over and listen to him play it. My dad was a whistler and he could whistle like a bird. I am often found walking the halls whistling or humming a tune and sometimes even singing. If I don't know the words, I make up my own.

I sang in chorus in school and in college and in the choir at three different churches and even sang in the choir at a Spokane church while my first husband was in the hospital for open heart surgery. I stayed with a family who sang in the choir. I enjoyed their hospitality when I was not at my husband's side.

When I was young, I wanted to be a composer. I played around on the piano making up tunes. I have never had lessons, but what I know was self taught. I practiced from the teach-yourself music book while my mother braided the sides of my hair and pulled it to the back. When I was a student at Lutheran Bible Institute, I wrote a song, but have not done anything with it. In the morning before I get out of bed, I grumble and groan to God about my aches and pains (see Romans 8:26-27), but after I get out of bed, I am singing hymns and songs of praise. What a great way to start the day followed by morning devotions.

Sewing

I started sewing at a young age (about 10 years old). The first thing I made was white flannel pajama bottoms for my teddy bear my grandmother gave me for Christmas when I was much younger. I took four years of home economics in high school and one in college. My first project in high school was a sleeveless dress with a bolero. My senior year, I made a wool coat. For extra credit, I remodeled and reupholstered my grandfather's easy chair. I cut the balls off of the open arms and webbed and padded them. I covered the ball legs with a flounce.

My freshman year of college I made a watermelon red wool suit with black velvet collar and sparkly black buttons. I entered it in the Make it Yourself with Wool Contest and won at district level.

Picture from front page of Yakima Hearld Society Section

I had fun receiving modeling lessons at state competition and won a lovely blue and white plaid yardage of Pendleton wool with which I made a fitted skirt with straps. Over the years, I have made several tailored wool suits. My most proud project was making my son a top coat out of my full-skirted coat. The gray wool fabric was reprocessed wool, so it had three lives. The only new parts of

YAKIMA VALLEY Junior College will be represented by Patricia Stilwell, left, and Jean Penney. Miss Stilwell will model a red tweed suit with velvet trim. Miss Penney's entry will be a brown wool crepe shirtmaker style dress.

the coat were the thread and interfacing. The lining and buttons, also, came from my coat. In college, I designed and made a dress.

There were many years I did not sew because of failing vision. After eye surgery, I thought I would give it a try and made a raincoat. I was surprised how well it turned out with its piping on sleeves and collar. I have made a few garments since, but got interested in making quilts. My sister used to volunteer at a quilt shop and has kept me supplied with fabric. I make quilts for the church bazaar with help and make crazy quilts with the scraps. A few years ago, I got acquainted with Alzheimer quilts and have made many of those to give away. I lead a quilting group at church and enjoy seeing what different people are working on and sharing ideas. Quilting has given me a purpose to live, as so many of the things I used to do are no longer on my plate. Mobility and flexibility issues no long make gardening and taking long walks feasible. Sew on!

Following are some devotionals published on the Peace Be With U website.

THE CUP

"I was thirsty and you gave me something to drink." Matthew 25:35b

This scripture came to mind one day when I was moving into a friend's apartment to stay there while she was in Alaska taking care of her grandchildren. I saw this man sitting near the entrance of the apartment. Several times I asked him if there was anything I could do for him on my many trips to the car. Finally I asked him if he would like a drink of water. He said, "Yes." So I brought him a cup of water. My next trip to the car I saw he was gone. I thought – Was this Christ? For he said, "Truly I tell you, just as you did it to one of the least of these who are members of my family, you did it to me." Matt. 25:40.

New Creation

Therefore, if any one is in Christ, he is a new creation; the old has passed away, behold, the new has come. II Corinthians 5:17 RSV

As I drive to and from church, I see many new houses replacing old ones, reminding me of the above scripture. I think: What was there before the old house was torn down? Is this how God thinks of our past–forgotten? In this new year we can think of what is ahead–not what is behind us. A life lived with Christ is a life with bright tomorrows. You can forget what is behind and "press on toward the goal to win the prize for which God has called (*you*)." *Philippians 3:14.* Praise God for new beginnings.

Even Me!

Fear not, therefore; you are of more value than many sparrows.

Matthew 10:31 (RSV)

The other day I was coming home to find the traffic stalled in the middle of the block. Being accustomed to delays, I patiently waited for the traffic to clear. As I waited, I noticed my lane was starting to move slowly, the oncoming traffic was not. Then I saw what it was all about. There was a little duck slowly crossing the street.

When I saw this I laughed and thought about the time I watched my son watching a tomato worm crossing a busy country road. Then I thought: Is this not like our heavenly Father watching and protecting his children on earth? The driver of the car could have knocked the duck asunder. But, no, it patiently chose to wait until the little duck could make up its mind where it wanted to go.

Is it not so with our heavenly Father? No matter how small, insignificant, and confused we feel. He is there to watch and protect us. To think we are that important to our heavenly Father, gives one hope our life is indeed worth living. Many times I feel alone and discouraged, and then God gives me another life experience with which I can witness for Him. Praise God for the saving grace He gives us in His son Jesus Christ. The life He gave for our sake, so we may have life. Glory hallelujah!

PRAYER: Dear heavenly Father, keep us always on the straight and narrow path. Let us not forget you care for us no matter how small and insignificant we feel. May we always be able to share your love by the way we live our lives. Amen

Thought for the Day: Let us not be discouraged. God does care and He has a place for each of us.

Journey to Glory

I will praise you, O Lord my God, with all my heart; I will glorify your name forever. For great is your love for me; you have delivered me from the depths of the grave.

Psalms 86:12-13 (NIV)

As I roll along to the celebration of the risen Christ, I see tulips marching along the fence and trees blooming in all their glory. The sun is shining to bring out the beauty in all of God's creation. I arrive at church to set in my usual front seat and wait for the sound of trumpets, brass instruments, bells and organ shouting the glory of the risen Christ. What a wonderful expression of the message of Christ in word, singing and visual images of Easter lilies and a projected picture of Christ. May the joyful message rest upon your heart all through the year. His is risen! He is risen indeed!

Prayer: May the glory of the risen Lord bring newness to your life with a closer journey with our Lord Jesus Christ. In the name of our risen Lord. Amen

Ever since joining the Edmonds United Methodist Church, I have been involved in some kind of Bible or book study to increase my knowledge and faith. This I will continue to do as long as I am able. I have come to love the Bible and God's Word. The church has become my family, of which many have walked with me on my faith journey. I know there are probably many more stories, but may leave them for later.

Patricia Beaudry

Patricia Beaudry is a long-time poet, who has been widowed twice, is a frequent contributor to Northwest Primetime monthly paper. She is happy to share with her readers her first book about her life and poetry.

Front cover art by **Ginger Carson**

Made in the USA
Columbia, SC
21 November 2017